PLAYWRITING:

A Manual for Beginners

PLAYWRITING:
A Manual for Beginners

by
DEBRA A. PETERSON

Dramatic Publishing
Woodstock, Illinois • London, England • Melbourne, Australia

Copyright © MCMXCIX by Debra A. Peterson

All rights reserved. No part of this publication may be reproduced or transmitted in any form or by any means, electronic or mechanical, including photocopy, recording, or any information storage and retrieval system, without permission in writing from the publisher.

Printed in the United States of America.
(PLAYWRITING: A MANUAL FOR BEGINNERS)

Cover design by Susan Carle

ISBN: 0-87129-822-8

Table of Contents

Introduction. vii

Chapter One: Can I Get Some Guidelines First?. 1
Chapter Two: What Do I Write About?. 7
Chapter Three: I Have an Idea: Now What? 11
Chapter Four: Creating Characters. 19
Chapter Five: Setting the Stage 23
Chapter Six: Getting Your Characters to Talk. 27
Chapter Seven: Playwrights Write Right 33
Chapter Eight: I Wrote a Play! What's Next? 39

Appendix One: Glossary 46
Appendix Two: Suggested Reading. 48
Appendix Three: Copyright Information 51

Introduction

So you want to write a play. Wonderful. But you're not quite sure where to start.

You know that a play usually takes place on a stage—although you may have seen plays performed in other places, say, a park or a barn.

You know that a play usually has at least two characters so they can talk to one another in *dialogue*. But then again, you may have seen a one-person play where the only *character* seems to be talking directly to the audience.

You may have attended plays with many special effects; or you may have attended a play where the most special effect was your elementary school teacher turning off the classroom lights.

As you can see, plays come in many styles. There is no single right way to write a play. But there are steps you can tackle one by one that will get you on the right track.

This handbook will teach you one way to write a play. The handbook includes four things that may help you over tough spots:

- a list of words that theater people use in the back of the book (words in this book that you can find in the glossary are *italicized*);
- exercises that can get you started with each step;
- suggestions that may help you complete each step as you go along;
- a suggested reading list.

Are you ready to begin? Good. Let's go.

Chapter One:
CAN I GET SOME GUIDELINES FIRST?

Some people like to know what they're getting themselves into before they begin a big project. This chapter will help you set up boundaries so your play doesn't get away from you.

Some beginning writers need to practice writing a scene before they attempt a play; exercises at the end of this chapter will help you do that if you'd like to test the waters before diving in. If you feel ready now, read on!

I. GUIDELINES

Your first play should be a one-act.

This play usually has fewer characters than a full-length play, so you don't have to keep the full lives of so many characters in mind. Also, a one-act play examines only one incident. It stays within a single time and place. It runs about 30 to 40 minutes. You have the time and space to develop it properly without worrying so much about the staging and technical problems that can give even a professional playwright a headache.

Your first play should be about an idea or issue that you care about.

If you care, your interest will keep you going when you're stuck; if you don't care, why write it?

Your first play needs *conflict*.

Somebody has to be fighting somebody else, or some thing, or some force to get what he or she wants. Include complications to keep the conflict alive. Conflict and complications are discussed in Chapter Three.

Your first play should be realistic.

You might be tempted to write a fantasy or an expressionistic drama for your first play. Hang on to that desire—but first master writing in a style that you're familiar with. Most television shows and movies are done in the realistic mode. You've probably seen realism more often than any other style. In your first journey into playwriting, keeping your challenges to a minimum by picking a style you know—realism—will allow you to concentrate on what's important: getting a good story, told well, on paper.

Writing in the realistic mode includes keeping your characters in a single setting and time. A one-act doesn't give you enough time to leap around in space and time; in addition, many contests require that the action transpire in a single setting. Stick to the ideal place and time for the action of the play. This lets you concentrate on the action.

Limit the number of actors needed to perform your play to three or four.

A play can have more than three characters, with each actor playing more than one part. This, however, can become hard to follow, both for you and for your audience. Remember: the longer a character stays onstage contributing to the action, the more interesting and lively both he and your script will be. Three or four characters is a good number for your first play. Fewer, and the audience may get sick of them; more, and you may have characters standing around with nothing to do or say. Your audience will wonder why they are there instead of focusing where you want them to focus—on the main action.

Make your characters emotional.

Let them feel strongly and let them show their feelings through actions. Your good guy should feel as strongly about what he wants as the bad guy feels about not letting him get it. Both should show how they feel through action.

Aim for a 30- to 40-minute play.

Why? For one thing, many contests require 25 pages (40 minutes). For another thing, writing toward this goal will give you room to grow and room to edit. Writing within a time limit also gives you room to develop characters and, at the same time, forces you to stay close to your main action.

How do you know how long it is? Reading it out loud is the best way. And you DO have to read it out loud, preferably with another person or in a cold reading (which is discussed in Chapter Eight). You get a shorter time when you read it silently. Another very rough way to gauge the length of your play is to *figure on one and one-half minutes of playing time for every page of dialogue.*

Introduce the action, the main plot, right away.

Sprinkle in *exposition, mood,* and *foreshadowing* after the play has gotten off to a lively start.

Don't let any one character talk for too long at one time.

Short speeches let all the characters take part in the life on stage. Short speeches increase the pace. How short is "short"? Limit yourself to one idea per speech, or about 20 words per speech, or "listen" to the other characters to see who wants to interrupt. Are there exceptions to this short-speech rule? Sure. You can write exceptions too—after you have this first play under your belt.

Keep going if you get stuck.

Work through problems. Get advice from other writers. Otherwise, you will have many great beginnings but no completed scripts.

Guidelines for your first play in review:

- Make it a one-act.
- Pick a subject you care about.
- Include conflict and complications.
- Make it realistic, sticking to one time and place.
- Limit the number of characters.
- Make the good guy and bad guy emotional characters prone toward action.
- Aim for a 30- to 40-minute play (about 25 pages).
- Start the action right away.
- Don't let a character talk for too long at one time.
- When the going gets tough, keep going.

II. EXERCISES

1. Write a one- or two-page argument between a mother and her teen-age child about a party. Don't let either character make the same point more than once. Stop writing the scene after both mother and teen-ager have made three good points. Read your scene out loud. Are you eager to

know what happens next? Or do you find yourself saying, "So what?" If your answer is "so what," rework the scene. Try adding a complication or a physical action.

2. Write a scene between a dissatisfied customer and a customer service representative. The customer wants to return an item to the store; the customer service representative wants the customer to keep the item. Now, rewrite the scene, throwing in a physical action for each point the characters make.

3. First, state your attitude toward a subject that you care about in one sentence. For example, "Love is not possible between two people who don't trust one another."

Second, turn this abstract statement into something concrete that involves characters and a situation, for example, "A man falls in love with a blind date but becomes suspicious when she won't tell him what she does for a living."

Next, create a character who cares a lot about this issue. In the example above, a character who would be concerned with trust might be a person whose last relationship fell apart because he was lied to. Give this character a name and a background. What is this character's goal? What obstacles are in his way? What does he plan to do to get around the obstacles?

Make a rough outline telling, in order, what happens. In the case above, the man might ask the woman where she works; he might snoop in her purse; he might try to trick her in conversation; he might ask another person what she does; he might wander around her home seeking clues; he might even follow her when she leaves her home on a Monday morning.

Chapter Two:

WHAT DO I WRITE ABOUT?

You need an idea before you can start writing a play. This chapter will suggest sources for basic ideas. After you get an idea, you will write an idea page, which is a one- or two-sentence description of what the play is about.

I. GETTING IDEAS

A **personal incident** is an incident from your life that might be a source for a play. Pick an incident that created strong feeling in you. Maybe you struggled with a difficult decision and finally had to make a choice. Maybe you expected an event to go a certain way and everything went wrong.

Another possible source for a play is a **dream**. Some dreams are unusually memorable because they are scary or bizarre. Have you ever said, "That dream would make a great movie"? It also might make a great play.

Character is where many playwrights start. They know—or they invent—a person so alive that he or she is a natural as the center of a play.

Some writers start with a **situation**: a family hiding from Nazis in an underground cavern realizes that the cavern's water table is rising. Or, a king who wants to retire gives everything to his children, and then he changes his mind.

Related to situation is the use of **newspapers and magazines** as sources for plays. How many times have you read a short newspaper article and said to yourself, "What a weird story! I wonder why a person would do something like that?" The writer takes such a story and invents the WHY of it. An example of a play that was created this way is *Equus* by Peter Shaffer. The playwright heard about a young man who deliberately blinded six horses, and he created a story to explain why someone would do such a horrible thing.

Another way to get an idea for a play is to decide its *theme*, that is, the play's message. If you want to tell your audience "Honesty is the best policy," figure out a situation that would show that; for example: Two boys steal a first-grader's lunch money every day until the first-grader's father finds out and reports the boys to the principal. The boys are punished.

You can make a play out of a **fairy tale**, a **myth**, or a **Bible story**. You can take an old folk tale and transform it into a play. Be sure this kind of a source is not copyrighted, or, if it is, be sure you get permission to adapt it (write to the publisher).

A friend or relative may have told you a strange thing that happened to her; that **friend's or relative's story** could be the starting point for a play.

II. THE IDEA PAGE

Once you have an idea for a play, write down what will happen in one or two sentences.

EXAMPLE: "This is a story about two teen-agers from feuding families whose love for one another is so great that they choose to die rather than be separated. Because of their deaths, their families stop feuding." (*Romeo and Juliet* by William Shakespeare)

EXAMPLE: "This is a story about a never-been-kissed young actress who discovers on her first opening night that she must kiss her obnoxious co-star in the last scene. But the person she really wants to kiss is her friend, who's playing the villain." (*Kiss?!?* by Nicole Johnson)

III. EXERCISES

1. Look through a magazine or a newspaper until you find three stories that interest you and that you feel have potential dramatic value. Write an idea page for each story.

2. Find a photograph that awakens your senses. It might be a person or a place or a thing. Write an idea page about the picture.

3. Ask a relative or a friend to tell you about the most interesting or bizarre or frightening thing that ever happened to him. Write an idea page.

4. Think of a person who is interesting to you. What is important to that person? How would that person react if she couldn't have what is important to her? Write an idea page.

Chapter Three:

I HAVE AN IDEA: NOW WHAT?

Now that you've gotten started, you can develop your idea. This chapter will help you do that by discussing *plot* and by providing guidelines to help you write a *scenario*. The exercise at the end will help limber up your imagination for writing your play.

I. PLOT AND CONFLICT

Plot is like the framework of a building. You don't see it when the building is finished, but the building wouldn't stand without it. Plot organizes the major actions of a play. Plot creates suspense. Plot forces characters to change and grow as they react to events. And if your characters don't change, you don't have a play.

Plot is conflict. Drama is drama because it shows characters in conflict: one person wants something and another person is trying to stop him from getting it. It wouldn't be interesting to watch a play where all the characters agree and everybody is working toward the same goal. But remember that conflict is more than characters bickering. Conflict causes changes in the direction a character is headed.

How do you create a plot? You begin at the beginning. The beginning of a play should do several things:

- **grab the audience's interest**
- **hint about things to come,** which will sustain interest

- **present the incident that gets the whole ball rolling,** called the *point of attack*
- **reveal the mood and style** of a play to the audience
- **establish the main characters,** either by actually having them on stage or by having other characters talk about them
- **reveal relationships** between characters
- **establish the** *setting,* or the time and place of the action

Think about *Romeo and Juliet*. The first three scenes fulfill all seven requirements. The first *scene* of this play shows a street brawl between servants loyal to the two feuding families, the Montagues and the Capulets. The audience sees via this brawl how deeply the two families hate one another. The first scene also introduces the main character, Romeo Montague, who is eager to love and be loved. In the second scene, Romeo decides to crash a party given by his enemies, the Capulets. In the third scene, the audience sees Juliet Capulet for the first time, and the audience learns that her parents are setting up a marriage for her. In only three scenes, Shakespeare creates interest: the audience knows Romeo and Juliet are sworn enemies, and it also knows that the two will meet shortly. What will happen?

Romeo and Juliet meet for the first time in scene five, which is the point of attack. *Romeo and Juliet* has begun, and the audience can't wait to see what will happen next. Answering the question "What will happen next?" brings us to the next part of a play: the middle.

The middle of a play is its heart. It shows the main character, the *protagonist,* trying to get what he wants while his foe, the *antagonist,* tries to stop him from getting it. In the middle of a play, the audience thinks the protagonist is about to achieve his goal, but then something happens to stop him. This happens time and again. The things that stop the protagonist are called *complications*.

A complication forces the protagonist to choose a different course of action, which causes the antagonist to change his strategy, too. In the middle of the play, there are surprises. There are discoveries. People come and go, and their actions affect the main character. **All complications should relate to the main action of the play.**

In *Romeo and Juliet,* for example, Tybalt's duel with Romeo complicates matters because Tybalt's death forces Romeo to leave Verona. Avoid conflicts that don't relate; it wouldn't matter, for example, if Juliet's mother and father had a fight about the party preparations—unless, of course, their fight prevented the party from occurring.

How do you know when your play needs a complication? When the play starts to get dull. When it doesn't seem to be going anywhere. When the characters seem to be spinning their wheels. When the protagonist seems to be close to getting what he wants.

How do you create a complication? When you write your scenario, which will be discussed in section two of this chapter, you will know the play's major conflict and the protagonist's goal. You should build in complications that slow or halt the protagonist's forward movement. You will want a complication that lasts longer than three pages, and it should be something that forces the protagonist to change his method of getting what he wants. Each complication should be relevant, and each should have its own climax—which propels the protagonist forward. Relevant complications move the action along until the protagonist is forced into a corner and must make a decision that will change the course of his life irrevocably. This point in the play is called the *climax*.

What's the difference between the climax of a complication and the actual climax of a play? The climax of a complication results in a change in direction for the protagonist; the climax of a play results in the protagonist either getting what he wants or not getting what he wants. The climax of a complication propels a play forward; the climax of the play propels a play to its end.

Imagine a man pushing a car up a hill. His goal, to reach the top of the hill, is complicated by his own physical weakness, his slipping on gravel, his fright when he sees a snake. He finally reaches the top of the hill and the car is poised to go down the other side. This high point is the climax of his journey. Once he gives the car a final push, his struggle is over.

A playwright builds a story toward just such a final moment. The climax is the highest point of interest in the play, the point where matters come to a head, the moment when the major conflict is decided, once and for all.

After the climax, it is time to end the play. This is called the *resolution*. This is where the universe of the play is returned to a state of balance. Whatever caused all the trouble in the first place is over, and it is time to let the audience relax. The resolution is short. It does not introduce new elements or characters. It does not "explain what it all meant." It does not jar the audience with a sudden change of mood. It does not leave the audience hanging. In *Romeo and Juliet*, the resolution of the play shows Romeo's father and Juliet's father shaking hands and agreeing to end the feud. No more need be said.

I Have an Idea: Now What?   15

II. THE SCENARIO

What is it? It is an outline of the play's action. It is critical to a play, because it keeps you from straying too far from your story. It shows you, before you begin, where you need to go. It prevents you from spending a lot of time writing material that you cannot use because it doesn't fit. It is, in short, as important to the playwright as the map is to the traveler. Don't start your play without it.

A scenario includes the following items:

- **Time and place of the action** (Setting)
- **Mode of presentation** (Style) Will your play be done on a proscenium stage, with the audience seated in one place facing the playing area, or will the audience be seated on three sides? Or all around? Will the audience be spoken to? Will the audience be directly involved?
- **Characters** A descriptive list of characters and how they contribute to the action.
- **Basic conflict** What is the central problem or tension that makes the play move forward?
- **Summary of the action** A list of major scenes that move the play along. What is a scene? It is a unit of action in a play where a point is made. Often, the action changes direction in a scene. At the end of a scene the audience should be anxious to find out what happens next.

How can you turn your idea page into a scenario? Do it the same way you do anything: one step at a time. On the next page is a chart that you can fill in, one way to write a scenario. You can see an example of a filled-in chart on the page after that.

Chapter Three:

WORKING TITLE:			
TIME AND PLACE	STYLE	CHARACTERS	BASIC CONFLICT

SUMMARY OF ACTION:

OPENING SCENE:

CLOSING SCENE:

I Have an Idea: Now What?

Example of filled-in scenario chart:

WORKING TITLE: *Romeo and Juliet*			
TIME AND PLACE Verona and Mantua 1400s	STYLE Realism	CHARACTERS Escalus Paris Capulet Montague Lady Montague Lady Capulet Romeo Tybalt Juliet Friar Lawrence Benvolio Minor characters	BASIC CONFLICT Two young people from feuding families fall in love, and they are so devoted to each other that they choose to die rather than give up one another.

SUMMARY OF ACTION:

OPENING SCENE: The marketplace. Two Capulet servants argue and then fight with two Montague servants. The fight turns into a public brawl. Prince Escalus enters and says that the next person to start a fight will be executed. Lord Montague asks Benvolio, Romeo's cousin, to find out why Romeo has been depressed lately. Benvolio finds out that Romeo loves a woman who doesn't love him back. Benvolio suggests that Romeo should check out other women.

SCENE TWO: Inside and outside Capulet's home. Count Paris tries to persuade Juliet's father that he should let Paris marry Juliet, Capulet's only child. Outside on the street, Benvolio and Romeo learn about a big party to take place at Capulet's house that night. Romeo and Benvolio decide to crash the party.

SCENE THREE: Inside the Capulets' house. Juliet learns that her parents want her to marry Paris. Juliet promises to look him over at the party.

SCENE FOUR: A street. Romeo and his friends, wearing disguises, joke as they walk to the Capulets' party. Romeo says he's had a premonition that something will happen at the party that will lead to his death.

SCENE FIVE: Inside the Capulets' house. The party is in full swing. Romeo and his friends enter. Romeo sees Juliet. Tybalt recognizes Romeo and wants Lord Capulet to kick him out. Capulet refuses. Romeo tries out his best pick-up line on Juliet, and he is both surprised and pleased when she gives witty answers to everything he says. They kiss. Juliet is called away. Romeo learns that Juliet is a Capulet. As he and his friends leave, Juliet learns from her nurse that Romeo is a Montague. THIS SCENE ENDS ACT I.

As you can see, by the end of Act I in *Romeo and Juliet*, the characters are in place and the scene is set for the unfolding of the action.

Now it is time for you to get some practice writing your scenario.

Using the chart on page 16 or a piece of scratch paper, write down your working title, time and place, style, characters, and basic conflict. Then, write a summary of scenes.

If you are stuck at this point because you don't know your characters well enough yet to know how they would react, read Chapter Four: CREATING CHARACTERS.

III. EXERCISE

Below are five dramatic situations. Pick one and write an opening scene for a play. Include action, even though the scene may not seem to call for it. Aim for a scene of at least four pages. Then, write a scenario for the rest of the play.

1. Two teen-agers plot a way to cut classes without getting caught.
2. Two runaways try to cross a busy highway.
3. A young saxophone player, completely devoted to his music, discovers a shy clarinet player slipping a note into his saxophone case.
4. Three teen-agers disappear from a shopping mall two days before Christmas.
5. A girl returns home on a Friday afternoon and finds nobody home and no car in the garage. Then she sees an envelope addressed to her on her pillow.

Chapter Four:
CREATING CHARACTERS

Drama is people-centered. People go to the theater to be entertained, to learn, to be moved. But those things happen for an audience because the people on the stage are interesting.

How can you create interesting characters? This chapter will help you by discussing character and by giving you exercises to get you started.

I. CHARACTER

Dramatic characters are drawn from life. Whose life? YOUR life. **Don't fall into the trap of creating a character that is a lot like a character you've seen somewhere else.** That's not creating. That's copying. Dramatic characters are built from your own memory, from people you've loved or hated, from hopes or failures in your own life, from your fantasies and daydreams. Once you create a character, he sometimes will decide for himself what he wants to do, and you can't make him do otherwise. If this happens, congratulate yourself: your character lives!

Another thing you must remember is that **a character in drama is a character in action.** An audience knows about a character by watching that character act or by watching the character react to what's going on around her. Sure, you can have another character report about something the main character did offstage, but an audience is most likely to believe something about a character if it SEES a character doing something that reinforces that belief.

Your characters have to feel. They can be intellectual, certainly, but first and foremost **they have to CARE about the play's topic.** And they have to care deeply. Strength of emotion gives a character hunger, a NEED to resolve his dilemma. Your main characters will go through extremes of emotion, and these extremes give your play life and motion. In addition, actors who have wide ranges of emotions to play will bring more energy to their roles. They will try harder to "get it right." This is to your advantage. Always remember: *If your characters do not care, your audience will not care either.* And if your audience does not care, it will not get involved and it will not connect with the central idea in your play.

Every character is in the play for a reason that relates directly to the subject and theme. Even a character's lifestyle should relate to the play. His emotions relate to it. And a character's emotions should be big enough or small enough to match the play's basic concept. If a character's emotions are too big for the play, the play will turn into a farce; if a character's emotions are too small for the play, the play will seem dull and its subject matter unimportant. Be sure to make it clear to actors who will play the characters in your script how big their characters need to be.

To really engage an audience, **a character in a play must face a crucial decision** that will affect the rest of his life, and maybe also the lives of others. In your play, you will put your main character in the position of having to make a choice. This choice will be directly related to your play's theme. Your character may even recognize that his decision has far-reaching consequences. This is called *discovery.*

Creating Characters 21

Your character will not be able to act unless she is motivated, and her action will match, in size, whatever motivated her to act. If a character tears her dress on a fence and reacts by murdering her date, you have a motivation and an action that don't match. Similarly, if a character's mother is injured in an accident and the character reacts by eating an ice cream cone, the motivation and action don't match. An audience must believe that your character would react the way he or she reacts.

Last, every character in your play should be interesting. If you think one of your characters is boring, your audience will think so too. Either eliminate the character or rewrite him so that he's interesting. And your main character should be not only interesting but also likable. Are all main characters likable? Of course not. But your first play is likelier to succeed if he is. Why? Because then an audience is more apt to care about the character's success in achieving his goal.

So, how do you go about creating a character? Know your character intimately. What is his favorite color? Has he ever skied? Did she attend college? What happened the first time she fell in love? Does he believe in life after death? Does he like natural or synthetic fabrics in his clothing? What does she do outside the life of your play?

The point of knowing details about your character is that the more you know, the more depth your characters will have. And the more depth they have, the more believable they will be. And the more believable they are, the more convincing they will be to an audience. And the more convincing they are, the likelier it is that your audience will get something from your play. And that's the point of writing, isn't it?

II. EXERCISES

1. List, in writing, the characteristics of someone you respect. List everything, even characteristics that aren't admirable. Then list, in writing, the characteristics of someone you like. Write a character sketch of at least two pages about a person who has all of these characteristics.

2. List, in writing, the characteristics of someone you do not respect at all. List everything, including characteristics that you would admire in someone else. Then, list, in writing, the characteristics of someone you actively dislike. Write a character sketch of at least two pages about a person who has all of these characteristics.

3. Look at the lists you generated for exercises one and two. Write a character sketch about someone who has characteristics from BOTH lists.

4. Look at the characters you created for exercises one and two. Create a situation that would pit these characters against one another. Try to write the scene so that each character's personality traits are revealed.

5. Examine characters in plays or movies. The character of Iago in Shakespeare's *Othello* is a classic antagonist. What makes him so evil? The character of Cyrano in Rostand's *Cyrano de Bergerac* is a classic protagonist. What makes him the perfect hero? What makes Darth Vader in the *Star Wars* series a bad guy? Why is Indiana Jones a good guy?

Chapter Five:

SETTING THE STAGE

You have a story. You have characters. Good. Now, let's take a look at the *setting*.

What is setting? It is the environment in which the action of the play takes place. You already know that a one-act play works best if it occurs in one place and one time, so what is left to say?

I. SETTING

You need to know right now that the setting you see in your head is probably NOT the setting that will make it to the stage. This is because theater is the most collaborative of the arts. Many artists contribute to the performance of a play. A scenic artist working with a director will design the world of your play.

As playwright, you can specify setting details that affect the action; for example, you can specify that the action takes place on a ship. You can specify the season or weather, IF the season or the weather affects the action. But if your script is overloaded with details about setting, chances are those details will be ignored by the other artists in the collaborative process.

What's a playwright to do?

First, you should know the setting top to bottom for the same reason you know your characters top to bottom. But just as every little detail about a character will not make it into the final version of your play, so every little detail about the setting will not. You have to know about the setting for YOU.

Second, you should know that there are five basic kinds of sets:

- **The box set.** This set uses the fourth-wall convention, so the audience seems to be looking through one wall of an interior room.
- **The outdoor set.** This set may use a scrim or a backdrop to suggest the sky or an outdoor locale.
- **The bare stage.** This set requires the actors to indicate place by their actions and dialogue.
- **The double house set.** This set shows two locales on the stage at the same time.
- **The special set.** This set will include any extraordinary setting like the rigging on a British naval vessel or Prospero's cave.

Whatever kind of set you decide will work for your play, remember: elements in the setting that are important to the action of the play should be described at the beginning of the play. A director or designer wants to know at the beginning of the play that there is an upstage window, especially if the main character escapes death by leaping out that window in the last scene. A play that requires a trapdoor will be problematic for a stage without trap space—and the designer or director will need all the extra time she can get to devise an alternative.

Setting the Stage

Next, be sure the setting you create gives your play enough room to BE. Could *Romeo and Juliet* take place in a living room? No. On the other hand, you should make sure your setting isn't so big that your characters get lost in it. Saroyan's *The Time of Your Life* would lose its punch if the audience saw the characters in their lives outside the barroom.

Finally, list elements in the setting that affect your five senses: sight, hearing, taste, touch, and smell. The exercises below may help.

II. EXERCISES

1. Think of a time in your life when you felt very strongly about what was going on around you. Maybe you were playing the last few minutes of an important ball game. Maybe it was a time when you had to tell your parents some bad news. List, in writing, as much as you can remember about what you saw, heard, tasted, touched, and smelled.

2. Look back at your idea page or your scenario. Have you selected a time and a place? Does the time and the place work BEST for the telling of your story? Would another place work better? Try one and see how the rest of the story plays. For example, if your play is set in a living room, try setting it on a porch or a front yard at night. Is it more interesting, or does the main character have more choices, or are more complications possible? Try another time. Does spring work better than winter? Does the sea-

son matter? Does 1964 work better than 1994? (If so, be sure to do plenty of research to avoid *anachronisms*.)

Remember: whatever makes your play more interesting, whatever makes the texture of your play more varied, whatever gives your characters more opportunity for action, is probably the best choice.

3. Read one of the plays listed in Appendix Two, for example, *The Man Who Came to Dinner* or *Equus* or *Hello Out There*. Find a place in the play where something is happening offstage. Then, write that scene as if it were happening onstage. Try to mirror the playwright's style.

Chapter Six:

GETTING YOUR CHARACTERS TO TALK

Dialogue and action are the two ways an audience comes to know the world of your play. You already know how important action is. Now, it's time for some pointers about dialogue.

I. DIALOGUE

The first, last, and in-between thing you have to remember about dialogue is that **your audience has to hear it.** In our homes, we use shorthand all the time because our family members understand our shorthand. Picture this: Bill comes home from school and the first thing his father says is, "Bill, what did I tell you last night?" Bill says, "Sorry, Dad, I forgot." Bill's father says, "Well, you missed it—and you know what that means."

Do YOU know what Bill's father means? No. In a play, an audience needs more. If we rewrote the dialogue above for a play, it might go like this: Bill comes home from school and the first thing his father says is, "Bill, what did I tell you last night about the garbage?" Bill's answer is, "Sorry, Dad, I forgot to put it out." Bill's father says, "Well, the truck went by today—and that means you have to haul our garbage to the dump."

Ah, NOW it's clear. It didn't take much adjustment; it only took a writer who kept in mind that she was writing for an audience. She didn't use shorthand that the audience couldn't know.

The second thing to remember about dialogue is that **whenever you can substitute an action for dialogue, do it.** Remember how important action is? Don't have a character say "I love you" when a kiss can make the same statement. Don't have a character say "I hate Jennifer" when you can show that character spray-painting graffiti on Jennifer's locker.

Third, remember that **dialogue is meant to be memorized by an actor.** An actor usually memorizes his lines by memorizing the *cue* that precedes his speech. If two actors are talking in a scene and one actor's response to every line is "You tell me," the other actor will have a terrible time memorizing his lines and delivering them in their proper order. It's a hard job, acting. Don't make it harder. Make sure you have no identical cue lines.

Fourth, **no play should consist totally of long or short speeches.** Short speeches increase the play's pace; long speeches slow it down. Long speeches should be used sparingly; save them for special moments. How do you know if a speech is too long? A speech should contain only one significant idea—if it contains more, it is long. If a character's speech makes another character want to interrupt but he is not allowed to do so, the first character's speech is too long.

II. DICTION

Diction is the way something is said. Some general rules apply:

Save the most important word or phrase or information for the end of the sentence. Believe it or not,

Getting Your Characters to Talk

each speech has a beginning, a middle, and an end. Of the three, the middle of a speech is the least strong. The beginning is stronger, and the end is strongest. For example, read these two phrases:

"Now, shut up, will you?"
"Will you shut up?"

Which is stronger? The second one. Why? *Because the final words are the ones that ring in the listener's ear and mind.*

If a word or phrase is not absolutely necessary, get rid of it. Realistic diction represents contemporary speech —it does not echo it. If it did, the modern theater would be drowning in "ya know?"s and "like"s. Train yourself to eliminate meaningless sounds.

The way a character talks should match who he is. Don't let a waitress who never finished high school talk like a college professor. (Certainly, such a thing is possible. Is it likely? No.) Force yourself to really listen to the way people talk. Write down what they say, or try to duplicate their speech (but NOT in their presence).

The way your characters talk sets the tone of your play. This applies whether your play is comic or tragic, light or dark. A character who says, "Gee, honey, whadja do that for?" conveys a different impression than that of a character who says, "How could you treat me in this detestable manner?" Your ear can hear the difference, which is why the next rule is critical.

Read your dialogue out loud. Your ear can hear clunky dialogue that your eye will slip right over.

III. EXERCISES

1. Write 10 lines of dialogue in response to each line below. Assume the character of the person to whom the first line is addressed:

    A. MOTHER: Just where do you think you're going dressed like that?

    B. TEACHER: I'm afraid that you've flunked the final exam, and that means you won't graduate.

    C: BROTHER: Look, man, do you really think you can hide that black eye from Mom?

    D. GIRLFRIEND: I swear it isn't what you think! I only wore his jacket because I was cold.

2. Pretend you are waiting in a bus station for a sudden thunderstorm to end so you can walk home. As you stand at the window, a person waiting for a bus strikes up a conversation. First, let the person be a middle-aged woman with a lap full of knitting. What do you two talk about? Next, let the bus passenger be a big man with a nasty facial scar, dressed all in black leather. What does he say to you? How do you respond? Last, try having a conversation with a scared seven-year-old boy who is riding the bus for the first time.

3. Go back to your scenario. Let your protagonist and your antagonist be trapped in a cave together. Don't let them talk about the events of your play—let them discuss ways to get out of the cave.

Chapter Seven:

PLAYWRIGHTS WRITE RIGHT

Everything you write has to be put in the correct format. A recipe is usually written with the ingredients first, followed by directions on how to put them together. A term paper has a very specific format. A play script is written in a form that makes it easy to follow, not only for readers but also for directors, actors, and scenic artists. This chapter will lay out a standard script format.

You can see examples of correctly done pages further on in this chapter.

I. SOME BASIC RULES

A play script is supposed to be bound, so leave a one-and-one-half-inch margin on the left. The right, top, and bottom margins are one inch. (This one-inch margin is standard on most word processors.)

The first three pages carry specific information, as follows:

Page 1: This is the title page. The title of the play is written in all capital letters, centered, about five inches down from the top of the sheet. It is underlined. Double-spaced under the title, also centered, is a brief statement about the play like "A one-act play" or "A verse play in two acts." This phrase is not underlined. It has only one capital letter, at the beginning. Do not use any punctuation.

Double-spaced under these two items is the word "by" followed by a single space, then the playwright's name, which is neither underlined nor written in all capital letters.

In the lower right corner is the playwright's name, mailing address, and phone number. Under that is copyright information, if it exists. (Copyright information is given in Appendix Three at the back of this book.)

Page 2: If the play is dedicated, that information appears on the second page. It is centered in the middle of the page. It is usually something simple, such as, "To Mom and Dad."

Page 3: The third page carries information about the play. "CAST OF CHARACTERS" should be centered, typed in capital letters, and underlined. After a double space, list the characters in the play and BRIEF descriptions of them. After a double space, the heading "TIME" is centered, typed in all capital letters, and underlined. After a double space, a brief statement of the time is given, such as "The play takes place on a rainy April day in 1874." After a double space, the heading "PLACE" is centered, typed in capital letters, and underlined. After a double space, a simple sentence about place is written, such as "The play takes place in the townhouse of Major Herringbone in Middlebury, Vt."

After you've typed these first three pages, some other rules apply to those that follow.

- Each page is numbered in the upper right corner. Along with each page number is a key word or two from the title of the play, for example, a page number in a script for Albee's *The Zoo Story* might read, "ZOO, p. 2."

- Stage directions containing information about producing the play (which will be read by designers, directors, operating crews, and performers) are kept to the right half of the page. Such directions are typed in italics (or underlined) and they begin in the middle of the page and go to the right margin. Capital letters are used to draw the attention of the appropriate theater personnel, such as "LIGHTING is subdued" or "THE CURTAIN RISES." The first stage directions will describe the environment, the mood, and the setting. It may take several paragraphs—but remember what was stated in Chapter Five: don't go overboard describing the setting; leave other artists room to create. Do not set off stage directions with parentheses.

- A character's name should be written in capital letters and centered on the page. Stage directions for the actor (such as how to say a line or where to go) are indented seven spaces from the left margin and are placed inside parentheses. Dialogue for the character is then indented five spaces (one tab) from the left margin. The dialogue ends five spaces before the right margin. Double space between speeches.

If a character's speech is carried over to the next page, the character's name is typed in all capital letters to start the dialogue, like this: "ROBERT (cont.)"

Now that you know the basics, it's time to write your play from your scenario. After it's finished, read Chapter Eight.

Break a pencil!

II. EXAMPLE OF A TITLE PAGE

<u>KISS?!?</u>

A one-act play

by
Nicole M. Johnson

Nicole M. Johnson
8188 Sunnyview Dr.
Eau Claire, WI 54701
(715) 555-1234

III. EXAMPLE OF A CHARACTER PAGE

CAST OF CHARACTERS

Ellen Foster: Freshman who has the leading female role in her school play and is apprehensive about having to kiss the senior she is playing opposite.

Scott O'Brien: Sophomore "friend" of Ellen's who tries to settle her nerves.

Gregory Briggs: Senior Ellen is playing opposite. He is very rude and uncompassionate about Ellen's fear.

Stacey Sullivan: Stage manager. Announces time remaining before the curtain rises.

TIME
The play takes place a half-hour before opening night in modern times.

PLACE
The play takes place in the girls' dressing room at Lawrence-West High School in Lawrence, Ohio.

IV. EXAMPLE OF A TYPED SCRIPT

KISS, p. 5

STACEY

> *STACEY enters from stage door with a clipboard, a headset over her ears, and a note.*

25 minutes till curtain. Oh, and Ellen, here's a note from Gavin.

> *STACEY hands her the note and leaves.*

ELLEN

Thanks, Stacey. From Gavin? What is the director doing giving us notes on Opening Night?

SCOTT

(Excited.)
Your first last minute Gavin note!

ELLEN

(Incredulous.)
Excuse me?

SCOTT

Last minute Gavin notes. You may have worked with him for a month, but you still can't fathom his unpredictability. Not till you've worked with him for a few years can you really start to understand his zany mind. He's been known to change entire scenes on Opening Night. What's this one say?

ELLEN

> *ELLEN quickly skims the note. Her eyes bulge. She reads it again and quickly shoves it in her pocket.*

(Nervously.)
Nothing much.

> *ELLEN sits again at the make-up table and pulls out her pony-tail. She pulls the brush through her hair as SCOTT comes over and stands over her.*

SCOTT

Come on, Ellen. What's so horrible that you're afraid to tell me?

Chapter Eight:

I WROTE A PLAY! WHAT'S NEXT?

What you just did is something nobody but you could have done. You created an entire universe out of your own imagination. But is it a finished play? The checklist below can help you answer that question. If you decide your play is not finished yet, one of the options discussed in part II may help you get it there. When you're satisfied that you've made your play as good as it can be, start sending it out.

I. CHECKLIST

Apply the following questions to your play. Be honest in your answers.

1. What is the climax of your play, and what leads up to it? If you can't precisely pinpoint the climax, your play still needs work.

2. Who is the central character—whose play is it? There must clearly be ONE DRIVING FORCE in the play, even if that driving force is not a person. If the play seems to be about one character at one point, and then switches so that it seems to be about another character, you need to clear up the confusion.

3. Chart every instance where two or more characters meet and interact on stage. Do you find that two characters who would strike sparks off one another never actually

connect on stage? Can you rework your play so the audience sees the fireworks when these two characters meet?

4. Have you set your play in the BEST place for the action to occur? If the setting is irrelevant to the action, you've shortchanged yourself and your play. There should be a reason *this* action occurs in *this* place.

5. Why does the action of the play happen now and not yesterday or tomorrow? Drama works because it presents a living action happening in the present; the audience lives the action along with the characters. Make sure your play must happen, could *only* happen, right here and right now.

6. Does your play take advantage of the unique format of live theater? Does the story work best as a play rather than as a short story or movie; that is, have you kept in mind the limitation of the playing space, the present-but-never-seen existence of a world offstage, the double presence of actors and characters, and the interaction of a live audience and live actors?

7. What is the play about? Can you state, in words, what aspect of human experience your play explores? Can you say "This is a play about the way people insulate themselves against emotional pain" or "This is a play about how lack of trust destroys love"? Distilling your play to its essence allows you to winnow out irrelevant material.

II. OPTIONS

The cold reading. This is unstaged and unrehearsed. It is the first read-through you do for a play that is to be performed for an audience. You need someone to read the stage directions and some actors. The main purpose of the cold reading is to let you hear the words you wrote being spoken.

Invite a few people to act as audience members. Be sure that you have enough complete scripts for all the people who will participate in the reading. Any room is fine for a cold reading: a classroom, a living room, an empty stage, if you can get one.

If the performers or the audience members want to give you feedback after the reading, accept it gracefully. DO NOT GET DEFENSIVE! Nobody says you have to implement the suggestions of others—and if you jump down the throat of the first person who criticizes your play, nobody else will want to say anything. That is too bad, because somebody in that room has something to say that will make your play better. Many cold readings include time for audience response. It also works to ask certain people ahead of time to sit on a panel. The panel, then, will discuss your play after it has been read. Invite the audience to listen.

In a classroom situation, plan for each writer to have about an hour for his 30-minute play's cold reading. Circulate scripts to everyone in the class a few days before the cold reading so everyone can pencil in questions or comments before they hear the play. Tell those people who have agreed to be actors a few days in advance what parts they will play.

On the day of the reading, set up a simple set with chairs or desks. Have the actors walk through their parts, scripts in hand. Audience members should keep their pencils handy so they can scribble questions or comments as the reading progresses, though they should try to watch the actors rather than read along as the actors perform the script. The playwright should read the stage directions.

When the reading is over, have everyone (including the playwright) sit in a circle. Start by asking "What works?" (not "What did you like" or "What was good?"). The goal is to improve the script, so comments should be phrased in a way that focuses attention on the play, not on its writer. Be kind in your criticism. "I don't understand why she runs away" is a lot easier for a writer to hear than "It's stupid when she runs away." The playwright is not allowed to speak until everyone else has spoken, although she can take notes.

At the end of the comment/question session, the playwright takes the floor for five to 10 minutes to answer questions and to explain choices that he made. At the end of the reading, workshop participants give the comment-filled scripts back to the writer so he can read their suggestions. After a couple of workshop sessions, everyone should be comfortable with this process and civil in his or her comments, because every writer knows by then that he or she will each sit in the hot seat.

In a well-run workshop, with an emphasis on courtesy, everyone's second drafts will be better after this first cold reading.

The **nonperformance workshop**. This usually is done after a cold reading, when you will have noticed that parts of your play need reworking. Contact a local theater group or a college theater department to see if they are interested in workshopping your script.

The structure of the workshop is flexible. The emphasis is NOT on performance. Instead, the emphasis is on working parts that aren't falling into place. If, for example, your play lacks depth, experienced actors can sometimes help you build in *subtext* by doing a series of improvisational exercises with your material. If you and the people in the workshop have time, it works well to have everyone gather for a day or two over a three- to five-week period. This allows you to do rewrites as the workshop progresses, thus giving you the opportunity to see your reworked script done by actors. Set a specific script-improvement goal for each session, and be sure to ask your workshoppers what feels right to them—they are, after all, actors, and actors usually have a good instinct about what will play and what will not.

The **staged reading**. This moves closer to an actual performance and usually requires 15 to 20 hours of rehearsal time. You need a director and actors. The actors move around on the stage, but they carry their scripts as they read the lines and perform the actions. Usually a simple setting is used (a table and chairs, for example). Sometimes props are used, usually only if they are critical to conveying the play's meaning. Even sound effects and lighting are used.

Many actors dislike staged readings because they take as long to produce as a fully staged play, but rehearsal time is cut short so actors don't have time to really get into their characters. In addition, stage movement—such as a kiss or a fist fight—is hampered when actors are still clutching scripts.

If you plan to invite an audience—say, 40 people—you must make it very clear that what the audience will see is a work in progress and NOT a finished performance. Have a question-and-answer session after the reading. Or, hand out a questionnaire before the reading that asks: What did you like? When were you confused? Was there anything you didn't like? What did you actively dislike? Were you bored? (If so, when?) Ask for other comments at the bottom of the questionnaire.

III. PLACES TO SEND YOUR PLAY

You can enter your play in a contest. A number of contests are held every year by groups or individuals looking for new plays. Contests are announced regularly in magazines such as *Writer's Digest*.

See *Writer's Market* published by Writer's Digest Books of Cincinnati for current markets. Other venues can be found in *Dramatists Sourcebook*, *Publisher's Weekly*, and *Stage Writers Handbook* by Dana Singer. An Internet search may also yield markets for your play.

Before you send off your play, however, read the following:

1. DO NOT SEND YOUR PLAY TO ANYONE UNTIL YOU ARE CERTAIN IT IS STAGEWORTHY.

2. Always include a self-addressed stamped envelope for the play's return. If you don't, you'll be considered an amateur.

3. Include a self-addressed stamped postcard. Clip it to the cover of your script. On it, write:

"We received your play today (date: _____) and we hope to let you know of our decision around (date: _____).
Signed _____."
This postcard will let you know that your play arrived safely.

4. NEVER send your only copy of a script.

5. Multiple submissions may be acceptable, especially since a group may take several months to reply. Write for submission guidelines if they aren't listed in your sourcebook.

6. It never hurts to send a query letter before you send your play.

Appendix One: GLOSSARY

anachronism – A person or thing that is chronologically out of place, especially if belonging to a former era but existing in the present (for example, Civil War soldier complaining about hippies).

antagonist – The character who stands in the way of the protagonist.

character – A personality as realized in a play.

climax – Point of highest dramatic tension; the turning point.

complication – Unexpected development in a play that changes the direction of the action.

conflict – Clash of opposing forces.

cue – Word, phrase, or action that signals to the actor that it is time for him to begin to speak or act.

dialogue – Conversation between two or more characters.

diction – The way something is said.

discovery – When a character first realizes the impact of his actions.

exposition – Material the audience needs to know about past actions that have led to the action of the play.

GLOSSARY

foreshadowing – A hint or clue about an event that will occur later in the play.

mood – Predominant emotional quality or spirit of a play.

plot – Plan of connected events that comprise the unfolding of a story.

point of attack – Moment in a play when the world of the play is unbalanced and the main action of a play starts; the first complication in a play.

protagonist – The person who is consciously striving to achieve a goal; the central character.

resolution – The point after the climax when the main action of the play is finished, the world of the play returns to a state of balance.

scenario – Plot outline; breakdown of the events of a play.

scene – A part of a play featuring a single action.

setting – The physical surroundings in which the action of the play occurs; the outer world of the play.

subtext – Emotional richness; that which is not said; that in a play which occurs *between* the lines or under the surface; what a character really thinks or feels as opposed to what he says out loud to the other characters.

theme – Subject or idea that a play is written to reveal.

Appendix Two: SUGGESTED READING

The trouble with listing recommended plays is that people want to know why you left *this* play off or included *that* play. My best advice is, "Just read every play you can get your hands on."

In case you can't do that, this list of plays is intended to get you started.

Full-length plays

> *And a Nightingale Sang* by C.P. Taylor
> *Anna Karenina* adapted by Helen Edmundson
> *The Cherry Orchard* by Anton Chekhov, translated by Elisaveta Lavrova
> *Cyrano de Bergerac* by Edmund Rostand
> *Death of a Salesman* by Arthur Miller
> *A Doll's House* by Henrik Ibsen
> *Equus* by Peter Shaffer
> *The Glass Menagerie* by Tennessee Williams
> *Good* by C.P. Taylor
> *The Importance of Being Earnest* by Oscar Wilde
> *King Lear* by William Shakespeare
> *Look Back in Anger* by John Osborne
> *The Man Who Came to Dinner* by George S. Kaufman and Moss Hart
> *The Mouse That Roared* adapted by Christopher Sergel
> *Nagasaki Dust* by W. Colin McKay
> *Ordinary People* by Nancy Pahl Gilsenan
> *Othello* by William Shakespeare
> *Our Country's Good* by Timberlake Wertenbaker
> *Our Town* by Thornton Wilder
> *Playing for Time* by Arthur Miller

Romeo and Juliet by William Shakespeare
The Time of Your Life by William Saroyan
To Kill a Mockingbird adapted by Christopher Sergel
Twelve Angry Men adapted by Sherman Sergel
What Price Glory? by Laurence Stallings and Maxwell Anderson
A Woman Called Truth by Sandra Fenichel Asher
The Zoo Story by Edward Albee

One-act Plays

Bury the Dead by Irwin Shaw
Fumed Oak by Noel Coward
Hello Out There by William Saroyan
Next by Terrence McNally
Visitor from Forest Hills by Neil Simon
Waiting for Lefty by Clifford Odets

Other recommended reading

Dramatists Sourcebook edited by Kathy Sova and Wendy Weiner
The Dramatist's Toolkit by Jeffrey Sweet
Stage Writers Handbook by Dana Singer
25 Ten-Minute Plays from Actors Theatre of Louisville, foreword by Jon Jory
Writing, Producing and Selling Your Play by Louis E. Catron

Single Copies of Plays

Write to:

Drama Book Shop
723 7th Ave.
New York, NY 10019

Dramatic Publishing
P.O. Box 129
Woodstock, IL 60098

The Fireside Theatre
Dept. ER-658
Garden City, NJ 11530

Samuel French, Inc.
45 W. 25th St.
New York, NY 10010

Theatre Arts Bookshop
405 W. 42nd St.
New York, NY 10036

Appendix Three: COPYRIGHT INFORMATION

Obtain form "PA" from the United States Copyright Office by writing to them at:

Library of Congress
Washington, DC 20559
Or, telephone: (202) 707-5000
(Leave your name and address on answering machine)

Class "PA" includes published and unpublished performing arts materials. They will send you a form, which you fill out and return along with a copy of the play and a check or money order for $20.

If you want other copyright information, address your letter to the Information and Publications Section at the Library of Congress.

When do you copyright? When your play is finished and you are ready to send copies out to producers. Note, however, that copyright registration is not a condition of protection, and book and play publishers always copyright their own publications. A detailed discussion can be found in *Stage Writers Handbook* by Dana Singer.